Not Your Grandmother's Flower Garden

A Strip-Pieced Quilt Method

by Marcia L. Baker

Dedicated to B. J. W.

Thanks to everyone at Country Calico's, Plano, TX, and Four Corners, Richardson, TX.

Individual thanks to Sally Anderson, Mary Beth Baker, Judy Benton, Karen Brown, Joan Ferell, Peggy Gray, Beverly Jones, Mary Lou Jones, Susan Maddox, Kitty Magrini, Lorrie Nugent, Lori Oliver, Helen Veniski, and Susan G. Wilson.

Also, thanks to The Cotton Club of Carrollton, TX, and The Bluebonnet Patches of Ennis, TX.

Special thanks to Jodi Campbell, Teri Everett, Sunny Lawrence, Sara Nephew, Sherry Searcy, and my family, Clint, Kevin, and Marcus.

Photography by Tony Bennett.

Cover design by Cece Hazelwood.

Printing by Tri-State Printing.

Copyright © 1996, Marcia L. Baker.

All rights reserved. No part of this book may be reproduced in any form without written permission from the publisher.

Every effort has been made to present accurate information. The publisher assumes no responsibility for errors in the text or illustrations.

Published by Alicia's Attic, 1609 Mullins Dr., Plano, TX, 75025-2866.

Printed in the United States of America

ISBN 0-9651439-0-2

New Address for Alicia's Attic
709 Knollwood Circle
Fort Collins, CO 80524-1585
(970)224-1336 FAX (970)224-1362

Table of Contents

Introduction 4

The Method 5

Supplies 5
Fabric 6
Quilting Basics 7
Overview of Process 7
Strip Pairs 7
Cutting Half-Hexagon Pairs 9
Cutting Half-Hexagon Singles 11
Laying Out the Design 12
Sewing the Top 12
Completing the Quilt 15

The Quilts 16

Just-A-Taste Placemats 16
Grandmother's Flower Garden 18
75 - Central, Shades Of Construction 22
Blue Diamonds 25
Mosaic Trip Around the World 29

Some Basics 34

How to use a Rotary Cutter, Ruler, and Mat 34
Basting 34
Quilting 35
Binding 35

Introduction

Quilting and sharing
Of hands and heart
Creating precious memories
In tradition and art.

                Marcia L. Baker, 1996

While writing this book, I thought about the balance necessary between quilting, friendships, and family. This poem reflects my interpretation of the need for our craft and art form. By expressing our ideas in fabric, we learn about ourselves and our relationships with others. My family and I have grown closer through the writing of this book and by my sharing the ideas and talent I have been given. I offer you these *seeds* which have our grandmothers' lineage, mixed with modern innovation, and hope you will *plant* them for future generations to cultivate and admire.

The quilt, *Mosaic Trip Around the World,* was originally being pieced with individual half-hexagon shapes. While laying out the design I was inspired to come up with a way to sew strips first, then cut. Progressively, I added more design variations. While discussing my ideas with other quilters, many commented that they liked the Grandmother's Flower Garden designs but would never consider making one because of the time commitment. Motivated by this and my passion for quilting, I decided to write this book.

You might be asking what's the trade-off? There is an extra seam and therefore more fabric is required. However, consider how early quilters pieced this quilt -- from their scrap bags. Did any of them consider the yardage required? Most likely not. I found that the extra yard or two is well worth the savings in time!

Supplies, fabric selection, and an overview of the process begin the first half of the book, *The Method*. Step-by-step instructions and illustrations show how the fast-piecing is accomplished. The second half, *The Quilts*, has the detailed information about each design. This includes a rating of 1(easy), 2 (average), or 3 (more involved), yardage tables with a selection of sizes, cutting and sewing requirements, diagrams of layout, and quilting suggestions.

As this process developed, I learned *tricks* which help with accuracy and speed. You will find these in the boxes throughout the text. Try some as you work on your project but choose whether to keep them or not. Only you can know what works best for you.

Watch how the quilt top *blooms*! I hope you enjoy this technique!

The Method

Starting out with the right tools and a few basics can make all the difference in how well a task moves along. This technique is no exception. Supplies, fabric, and an overview of the method begin this section. The step-by-step instructions lead through the process and refer to the specific project information as necessary.

Supplies

You will need the following:

Sewing machine with basic accessories. i.e. scissors, pins, seam ripper, etc.

Rotary cutter, acrylic ruler and mat

8" Clearview™ Triangle, Figure 1. Other 60 degree rulers can be used but the rule lines may be drawn from a different reference point.

Thread. I recommend a medium gray because all of the fabrics, light, medium and dark, are sewn in one seam at some point in the design.

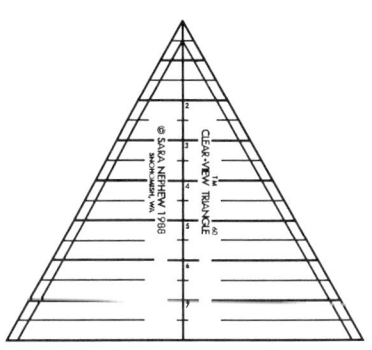

Figure 1 *Clearview™ Triangle*

Order from:
   Clearview Triangle
   8311 180th St. S.E.
   Snohomish, WA 98290

HINT: Inspiring Future Quilters

Ask your local preschool if they would like the fabric scraps from your projects. Even the thin trimmings from the first rotary cut are great. The children love the colors and textures and can use their imaginations to make a collage or to decorate a wonderful creation! Do you remember fabric being a part of your early childhood?!

The Method

Fabric

Use 100% cotton fabrics. The yardage required is listed in the table for each individual project. These amounts allow for straightening the fabric and some shrinkage, but no extra cuts. Add $1/8$ to $1/4$ yd if you need it for peace of mind.

Select fabrics which are solid looking in values ranging from light to medium to dark. Small to medium size prints are best because the pieces are finished to the size in Figure 2. If there is too much variation in a fabric, the hexagon pattern can be lost.

> *HINT: Selecting the Fabric*
>
> *Make a viewing template by tracing the shape in Figure 2 to paper. Place this drawing over black construction paper and trace again with some pressure. Cut out the shape leaving a window to view through. Place this on the fabrics you are considering, to see how the fabric will look when pieced.*

Figure 2
Finished Size of Fabric Pieces

For each design, the greater the difference between light, medium, and dark, the more distinct the patterns will be. Suggested values are given in the diagrams for each project. To get a better idea of what a particular color/value combination does, use colored pencils to shade a copy of the design grid from the inside front cover.

If desired, wash the fabrics the way you intend to wash the finished project, e.g. wash quilt fabrics with Orvus in luke warm water. This is a cleanser which can be purchased at your local quilt shop or feed store. The placemats will probably be thrown in with the regular laundry, so wash the material that way from the beginning.

The Method

Quilting Basics

Always sew with $1/4$" seam unless stated otherwise. If you need directions for basic quilting methods such as rotary cutting, basting, quilting or binding, read the section "Some Basics."

Overview of Process

In teaching classes, I have found it helpful to show the students the basic steps before actually sewing. This is an overview of the piecing process:

Three-inch-wide strips of fabric are sewn together to make strip pairs. Figure 3a. These are then cut into pieces called half-hexagon pairs. Figure 3b. From other strips, half-hexagon singles are cut. The design is arranged from the half-hexagon pairs and singles. Figure 3c. These pieces are sewn into rows. The rows are assembled resulting in an easily-pieced hexagonal quilt top. Figure 3d.

Strip Pairs

Cut the 3", $1\,5/8$", and binding strips as listed in the table for the project. Not all projects require the $1\,5/8$" strips.

The 3" strips are cut 45" long for the full width of fabric. If the lengths listed are 22", 15", or 11", fold the 3" strip into halves, thirds, or fourths, respectively. Cut with scissors at the fold. **Do not cut the lengths to these exact measurements.** They are only approximations since fabric widths vary so much.

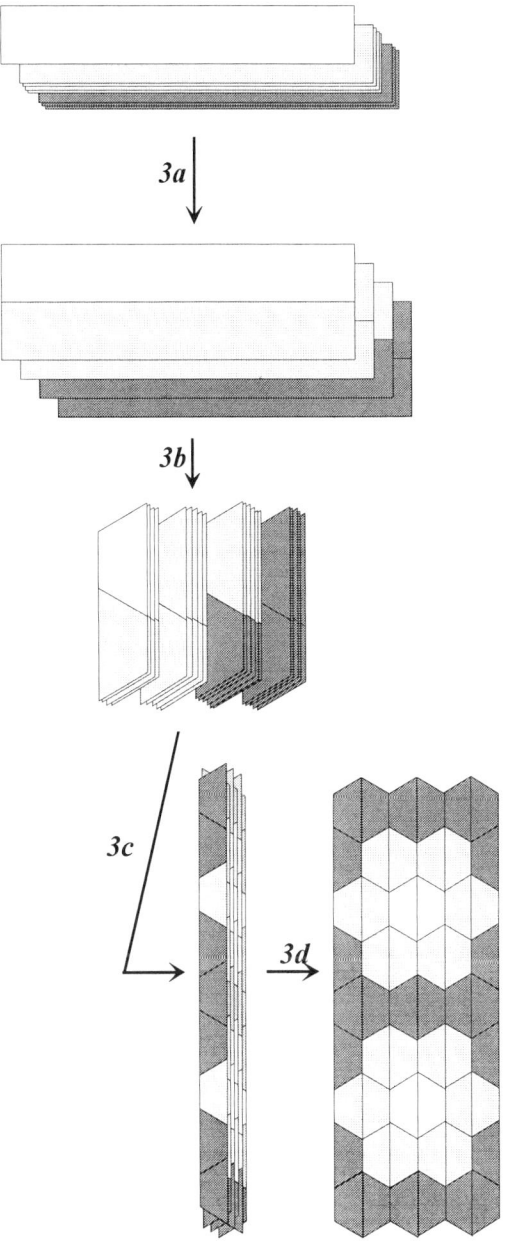

The Method

Sew the 3" strips into strip pairs as specified in "The Quilts" section for your project. The ends will probably not match and that is okay. It will be trimmed later.

> *HINT: Making It Accurate*
>
> *With this technique, it is important to have a consistent $1/4$" seam. Check your first seam by measuring the width in several places. Two 3" strips sewn together should be $5 1/2$".*

Press the strip pairs with the seam allowance toward the darker fabric.

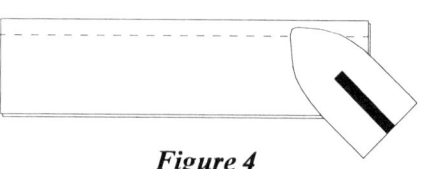

Figure 4

> *HINT: Pressing the Seams*
>
> *When working with long seams, as in this method, press the seams flat before opening them. Figure 4. This gets all of the fabric going one direction making it easier to control.*
>
> *To press the seam open, place the strip which will have the seam allowance pressed away from it, wrong side down. Gently lift the other strip up with your hand, keeping the seam allowance flat on the ironing surface. Use the edge of the iron to press the seam open. Figure 5. Avoid pulling on the fabric as this will stretch it. Pick up the iron and move it to the next section to keep from pressing in wrinkles.*
>
> *With or without steam, let the iron do the pressing. (I prefer steam.)*

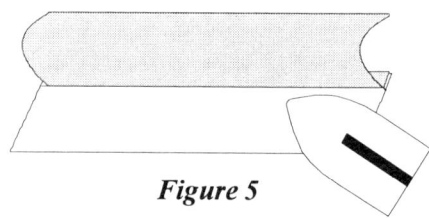

Figure 5

Cutting Half-Hexagon Pairs

From the strip pairs are cut half-hexagon pairs. (Figure 6) All of the designs are made from this one unit. Cut as many half-hexagon pairs as you can from each strip pair (about 10 from 22" wide and 20 from 44" wide.) If one or two half-hexagon pairs are cut wrong, don't worry because there are a few extras.

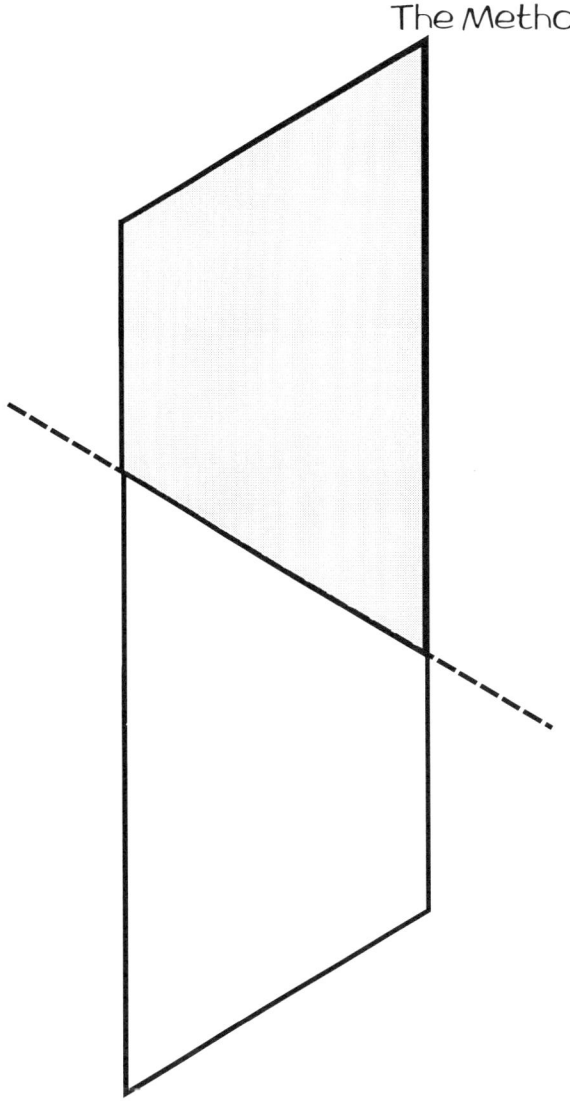

Cut the half-hexagon pairs from the strip pairs by following steps 1- 3 below. Check the first half-hexagon pair with Figure 6 before cutting all of them.

Figure 6 *Half-Hexagon Pair, actual size. If the first one does not match, see bottom of page 10.*

1. Align the triangle at the right end with point up and rule lines matching the seam line. Cut on the right side of the triangle. (Figure 7) Note: The strip can be placed with either fabric at the top.

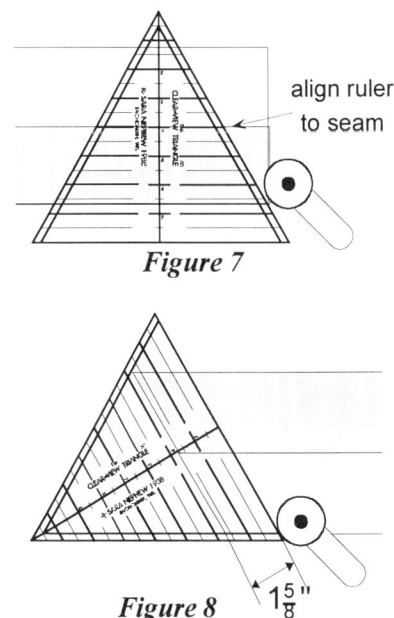

2. Turn the strip pair with the angled end to the left. Align $1/4$" seam allowance of ruler along the bottom edge of the strip. Cut $1\ 5/8$" wide strips. (Figure 8) When the ruler does not align with the bottom edge (most likely after 4 - 5 cuts), recut the angle as in step 1 above. (Figure 7)

Not Your Grandmother's Flower Garden

The Method

3. Lay the 1 5/8" strip lengthwise, left to right. Cut a triangle off the right end by aligning the 3" mark at the bottom and the 1/4" mark on the center seam line. (Figure 9) Cut the other end the same way. (Figure 10)

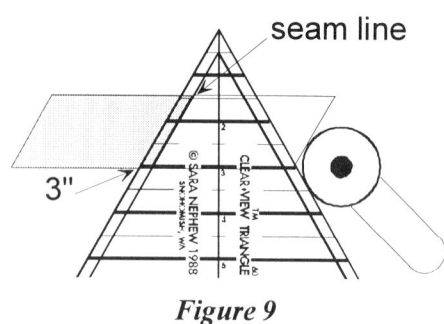

Figure 9

HINT: Making It Faster *

Layer two sets together, both right-side up, with seam allowance going in opposite directions. Then cut.

*Only recommended for those with advanced rotary cutting experience.

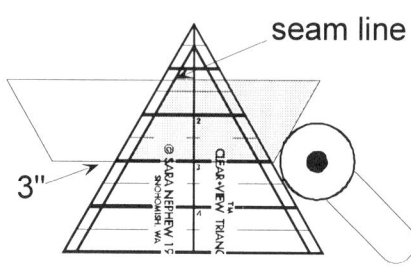

Figure 10

HINT: Making It Faster

For speed, cut several 1 5/8" strips from the strip pair (Step 2). Lay them out. Then cut off the triangles (Step 3).

If the Half-Hexagon Pair doesn't match:

- Check strip pair widths, is 3" + 3" sewn 5 1/2"?
- Before cutting 1 5/8" strip from the strip pair, was the angle cut?
- Is 3" on ruler actually 3" from top point?
- Was the 1/4" line on the seam when cutting off triangles?

- If the half-hexagon pair matches Figure 2 except it is wrong-side up, then the starting angle was cut with triangle point down or on the left side of the ruler. If you have cut everything this way, it will be okay. Just be sure to start all strips the same way.

The Method

Cutting Half-Hexagon Singles

For Just-A-Taste, Grandmother's Flower Garden, and Blue Diamonds, the sides of the quilt are filled with individual half-hexagons. Use the 1 5/8" strips listed in the project table. Align the triangle at the right end with the point up and rule lines matching the cut edges. Cut on the right side of the triangle. Figure 11.

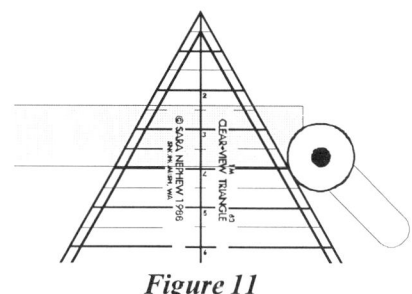

Figure 11

Turn strip with angled end to the left. Align the ruler, point down, with left edges matching and 3" mark along the top edge of strip. Cut one half-hexagon. Figure 12.

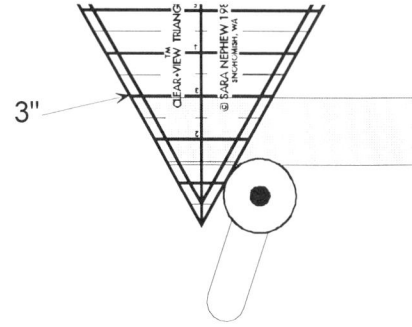

Figure 12

Rotate the ruler, point up, with the left edges matching and the 3" mark along the bottom edge of strip. Cut another half-hexagon. Figure 13. Continue rotating the ruler and cutting half-hexagon singles from the entire strip.

Note: These single half-hexagons are straight of grain and do not ease as readily as the pairs which are bias.

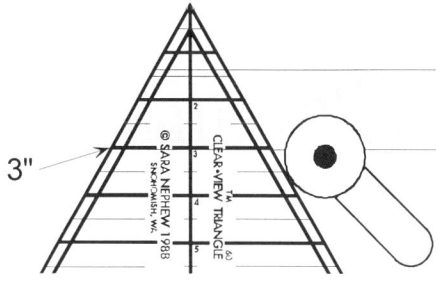

Figure 13

HINT: Keeping It Together

Resealable plastic bags work great to keep these different pieces separated, stacked, clean, and less likely to be frayed. I use them often because I usually have several projects going at once and can easily grab what I need when I need it.

The Method

Laying Out the Design

Using the diagrams for the selected project from "The Quilts" section, place the half-hexagon pieces into the desired arrangement.

If you want a random effect, check for any patterns which might be emerging. i.e. similar colors in a line, too many or too few of one color in a particular section of the quilt, etc. When finished arranging, take a picture with a camera, sketch the layout, or color a design page (copy from inside front cover), so you can refer to it later as you are sewing.

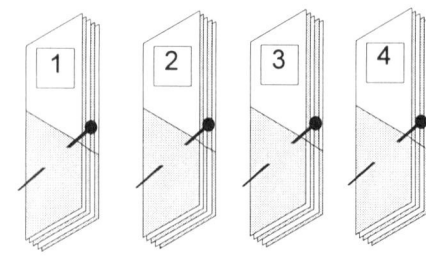

Figure 14

I recommend labeling the top of each row, stacking the pieces, and pinning them together. Then you can sew one row at a time without taking up a large space. Figure 14. However, if you have the room, you may choose to leave the pieces laid out as you work. Do what is most comfortable and works best for you.

Sewing the Top

Preview this whole section before actually sewing any seams. I have included tips which can help the points be more accurate with fewer headaches. (I have already had the headaches for you.)

Sew the half-hexagon pairs and singles into rows, using $1/4$" seams as shown in Figure 15. With right sides together, align the edges having the pieces cross where the seam line will be. Slide the pieces back and forth until the "ears" are the right size according to Figure 16 which is actual size for this seam.

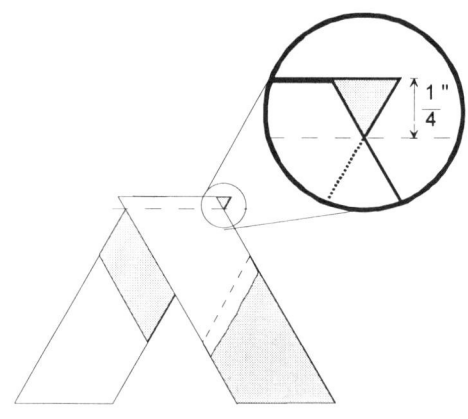

Figure 15

> HINT: Learning a New Angle
>
> Make a template of Figure 16 using see-through plastic. Use this to check alignment while you are sewing until you are familiar with the $1/4$" ears.

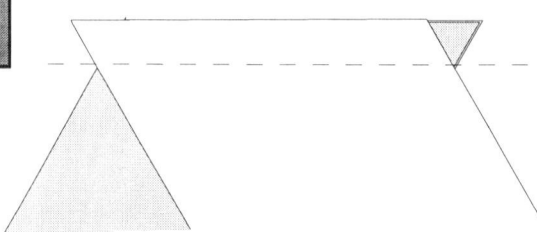

Figure 16
Not Your Grandmother's Flower Garden

The Method

After sewing a few and checking them, you will be more comfortable with this new angle. Figure 17 and Figure 18 show what happens when the "ears" are too big or too small, respectively.

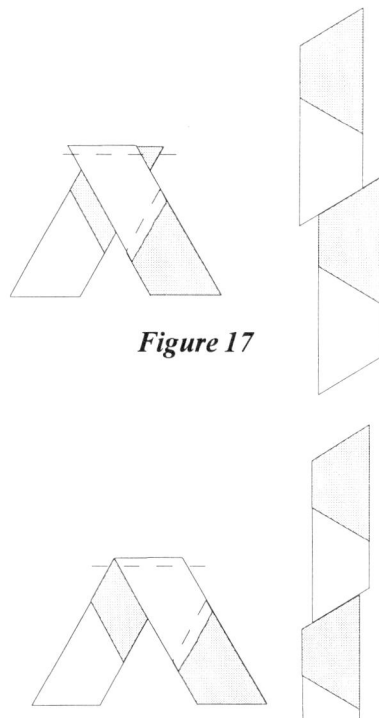

Figure 17

Figure 18

> *HINT: Chain Piecing*
>
> *Chain piecing makes sewing faster and saves thread. To chain piece, sew one seam taking 2 or 3 stitches beyond the fabric. Then insert the next seam to be sewn without removing or clipping the threads from the previous seam. Continue in this manner until all seams are sewn for one row or unit.*

Notice that these pieces can be sewn together in any order so it is important to keep them straight! I use the following method: With the stack vertical, pick up the first pair with one hand (always using the same hand), hold it at the top of the next pair, and flip it down putting right sides together. Figure 19.

Sew the first two pieces together. Then sew the next two pieces, etc. The sets of two half-hexagon pairs can then be sewn together into sets of four, and finally into the complete row.

Check that the pieces are in the correct order by comparing them to the previously sewn row or to the photo or design page made when laying out the quilt.

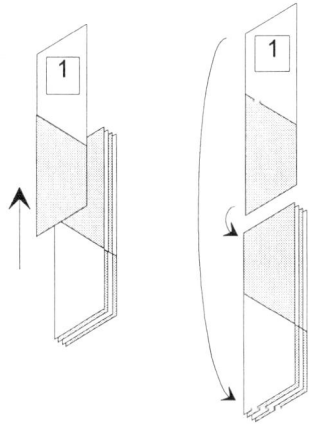

Figure 19

> *HINT: Saving Time and Thread*
>
> *Use a shim when chain piecing. Cut (2) pieces of scrap fabric approximately 2" square. Feed this in when you are at the end of a group of seams. Sew across it and stop. Clip the group off from the back of the shim. I use this all the time to eliminate those aggravating long threads which constantly need to be clipped. This takes a while to get into a habit but it is well worth the effort!*

The Method

Once all of the rows are sewn, press **all** seams in a row in one direction. Press the next row the opposite direction. i.e. Press the first row up, the second row down, third row up, etc. Figure 20. Note: Some seams will be pressed opposite of the original pressing. Be careful not to stretch the rows when pressing them.

> *HINT: Pressing Up or Down ?!*
>
> *If pressing the seams up, hold the top of the row in your left hand. From the right side, have the seam laying flat then use the iron to press back the fabric. Similar to Figure 5. If pressing the seams down, hold the bottom of the row in your left hand.*

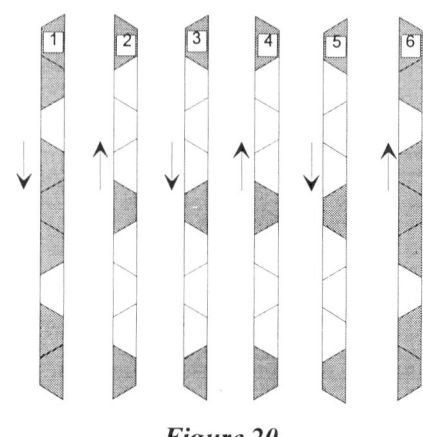

Figure 20

To sew the rows together, place right sides together making sure which edges of the rows should be sewn together. The seams will line up on either edge but the fabric matches only on one edge. Align the seams so they lock. Figure 21. Ease as needed between seams.

Press the seams closed first, then press open as described with the strip pairs, Figures 4 and 5. Sew in sets of two, press, and then sew these sets together. Figure 22. Working with one long seam at a time is easier than trying to press the entire quilt all at once.

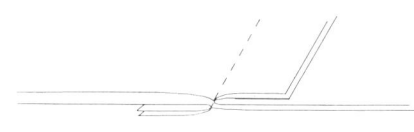

Figure 21

For Grandmother's Flower Garden and Blue Diamonds, attach borders as described on the project pages. On all of the designs, I recommend stay-stitching around the edge of the quilt to keep the bias edges from stretching. For straight edges, stay-stitch slightly outside the line where the binding will be sewn. Then trim off the jagged hexagon edges leaving $1/4$" seam allowance. If you plan on finishing the edge with a hexagonal shape, stay-stitch following the hexagon shapes.

You now have a hexagonal quilt top pieced the easy way, and it is definitely not your Grandmother's Flower Garden!

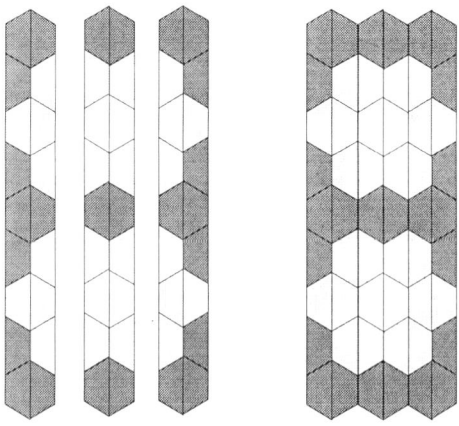

Figure 22

Completing the Quilt

See the diagram in "The Quilts" section to determine how to sew the backing. Measure the quilt top to make sure yours is close in size to the finished size listed. The backing yardage given allows at least three inches extra on each side. Divide the backing yardage into the appropriate number of pieces. Trim selvages off each edge. Sew together with $1/2$" seams. Press seam flat then open.

Before basting and quilting, consider how you want to finish the edges. Binding, which is done after quilting, can be used for straight or hexagonal edges. Another way to get the hexagonal edge is to finish similar to a pillow. Baste the top and backing with right sides together and the batting on the outside, top or bottom. Sew through all three layers leaving an opening for turning. The larger the quilt, the larger the opening needs to be. Turn and slipstitch opening. Then spread the quilt out, eliminating any wrinkles, re-baste and quilt. This may seem time consuming, but can provide a simple, elegant finish to the quilt.

Traditionally, these patterns are quilted $1/4$" inside each hexagon, or $1/4$" outside the flower or diamond shape. Figures 23. The former is the pattern using the smaller dashed lines. The latter is the larger dashes with the center hexagon quilted.

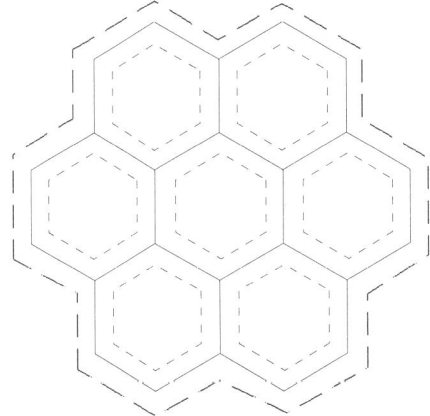

Figure 23

The quilting patterns used for the quilts shown on the cover are given for suggestions and inspiration. All of these were machine quilted without marking. The short sides of the hexagons, $1\,1/4$", lend themselves to using the shapes as guides while quilting. Hand quilting works just as well, if you prefer. I am currently hand quilting a queen size quilt and enjoy the variety and tranquility it offers, a relaxing pastime that our grandmothers enjoyed.

Use leftover half-hexagons to sew an extra flower, diamond, or single hexagon. Applique to the back for a label. Or sign and date the front with pigma pen.

I have enjoyed sharing this technique with you! It will be exciting to see the *gardens* that grow from these *seeds*!

The Quilts

Just-A-Taste Placemats

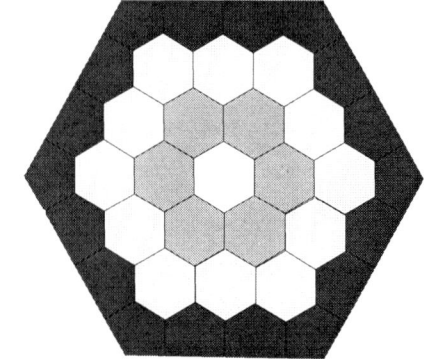

Not quite sure if this technique is for you? Get just a taste of the method while making these simple placemats. This project is great for beginners and for gift-giving. Have fun trying something new with fancy fabrics or whimsical prints. Read through the instructions in "The Method" section. As needed, use Table 1, the layout diagram, and quilting designs shown for this project.

Table 1 Just-A-Taste Placemats

4 Placemats	15" x 13.5" each					
YARDAGE Only allows for shrinkage and straightening.	Center	1st Ring	2nd Ring	3rd Ring	Binding	Backing
	1/8	1/3	5/8	3/4	3/8	1
CUTTING Cut number of strips in parentheses. 22" is approximate.						
	(1) 3" x 22"	(4) 3" x 22" (1) 3" x 45"	(1) 3" x 22" (5) 3" x 45"	(2) 3" x 22" (4) 3" x 45" (4) 1 5/8" x 45"	(6) 2" x 45"	

	Strip Pairs to Sew	# Half-Hex Pairs to Cut	# Half-Hex Singles to Cut
Center to 1st Ring	(1) 22" pair	8	56 from 1 5/8" strips of 3rd Ring
1st Ring to 1st Ring	(1) 22" pair	8	
1st Ring to 2nd Ring	(1) 22" pair (1) 45" pair	24	
2nd Ring to 2nd Ring	(1) 45" pair	16	
2nd Ring to 3rd Ring	(2) 45" pairs	40	
3rd Ring to 3rd Ring	(1) 22" pair (1) 45" pair	24	

Layout

Layout one placemat using Figure 24. Sew it together following the instructions in the method section. After piecing the entire placemat, staystitch each side just inside where it will be trimmed. Trim the edges along the points as shown.

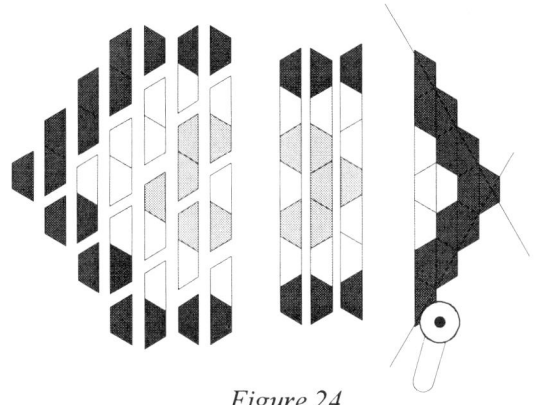

Figure 24

Quilting Designs

Figure 25 shows some ideas for quilting designs. Traditionally the flowers are quilted 1/4" away in each hexagon or as a whole flower. These are great for practicing machine quilting.

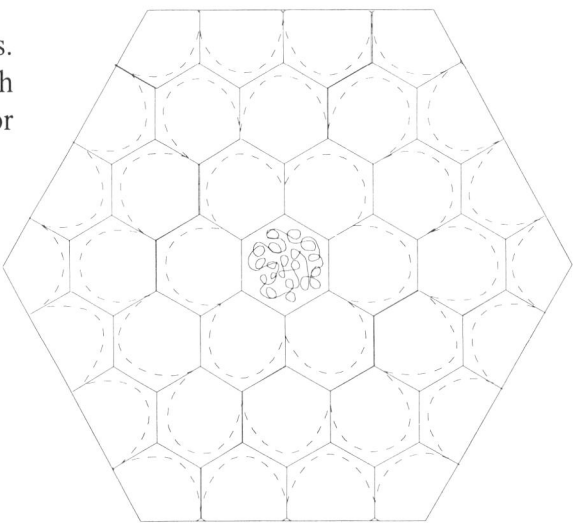

Figure 25

Binding

Because of the hexagonal angles, the binding is sewn and folded differently than a right angle. The section "Some Basics" provides binding instructions for mitering corners. To miter these larger angles, when sewing off at a diagonal as in Figure 54, sew a diagonal which divides the larger angle in half. Fold back along the sewn diagonal line. Fold the binding down, aligning the loose binding with the next edge to be sewn. This is similar to Figure 56, in that the new fold is still perpendicular to the edge about to be sewn. However, the previously sewn binding, angles out o the right of the new fold.

Grandmother's Flower Garden

Recreate this quilt with soft, pastel colors or choose bright, dramatic ones as shown on the cover. Whichever you select, you will be surprised at how fast the garden grows. To make this quilt, follow the instructions in the section titled "The Method." Use Table 2, the layout diagrams, and the special instructions included here when directed.

Table 2 Grandmother's Flower Garden

		CRIB	LAP	TWIN	FULL/QUEEN	KING
Finished Size		35" x 45"	51" x 73"	66" x 87"	89" x 101"	106" x 101"
Number of Flowers		13	41	72	124	150
YARDAGE		Only allows for shrinkage and straightening.				
Center		1/3	2/3	7/8	1 1/4	1 1/2
(Number of Flower Fabrics) Yards of Each		(5) 1/3 ea.	(14) 1/3 ea.	(8) 2/3 ea.	(14) 2/3 ea.	(17) 2/3 ea.
Background		2 1/8	4 1/8	5 3/4	10	11
Binding		1/3	1/2	5/8	3/4	7/8
Backing		1 1/2	3 1/4	5 1/3	8	9
CUTTING		Cut number of strips in parentheses. 22" is approximate.				
Center		(6) 3" x 22"	(14) 3" x 22"	(8) 3" x 45"	(14) 3" x 45"	(17) 3" x 45"
Flowers, each fabric		(1) 3" x 45" (4) 3" x 22"	(1) 3" x 45" (4) 3" x 22"	(7) 3" x 45"	(7) 3" x 45"	(7) 3" x 45"
Background		(9) 3" x 45" (8) 3" x 22"	(26) 3" x 45" (16) 3" x 22"	(54) 3" x 45"	(88) 3" x 45"	(106) 3" x 45"
Background (singles)		(2) 1 5/8"x45"	(4) 1 5/8"x45"	(4) 1 5/8"x45"	(5) 1 5/8"x45"	(5) 1 5/8"x45"
Background (border)		(8) 1 3/4" x 45"	(12) 1 3/4" x 45"	(18) 1 3/4" x 45"	(22) 1 3/4" x 45"	(24) 1 3/4" x 45"
Binding		(4) 2 1/4"x45"	(6) 2 1/4"x45"	(9) 2 1/4"x45"	(11) 2 1/4"x45"	(12) 2 1/4"x45"

Table 2 Grandmother's Flower Garden (continued)

	CRIB	LAP	TWIN	FULL/QUEEN	KING
SEWING STRIP PAIRS	Sew number of pairs in parentheses of lengths listed.				
center to flower	(1) 22"	(1) 22"	(1) 45"	(1) 45"	(1) 45"
each flower to itself	(1) 22"	(1) 22"	(1) 45"	(1) 45"	(1) 45"
each flower to background	(1) 45" (1) 22"	(1) 45" (1) 22"	(4) 45"	(4) 45"	(4) 45"
background to background	(2) 45" (1) 22"	(6) 45" (1) 22"	(11) 45"	(16) 45"	(19) 45"
BORDERS					
# of side border hexagons	9	16	20	23	23
# of top border hexagons	7	11	15	21	24
BACKING					

Layout

Grandmother's Flower Garden has a basic "block" which is repeated throughout the entire quilt top. Layout one flower following Figure 26. The flowers fit together like a dovetail joint (as in woodworking) or jigsaw puzzle pieces. Figure 27. This method is different in that the "blocks" are not sewn together but are used only for designing. Use the half-hexagon singles to fill in the edges. The rows are sewn into strips which lay the width of the quilt, as shown in the upper left hand corner of Figure 28. On sizes smaller than king, the flowers on the right side which appear to be cut in half should be replaced with background pieces, making the right edge similar to the left edge of the quilt.

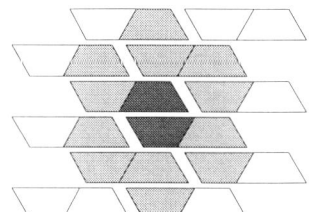

Figure 26

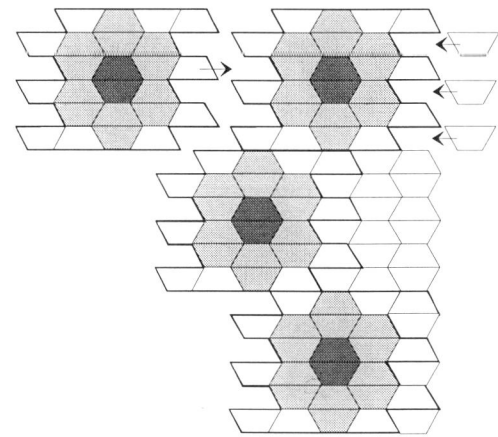

Figure 27

The Quilts. Grandmother's Flower Garden

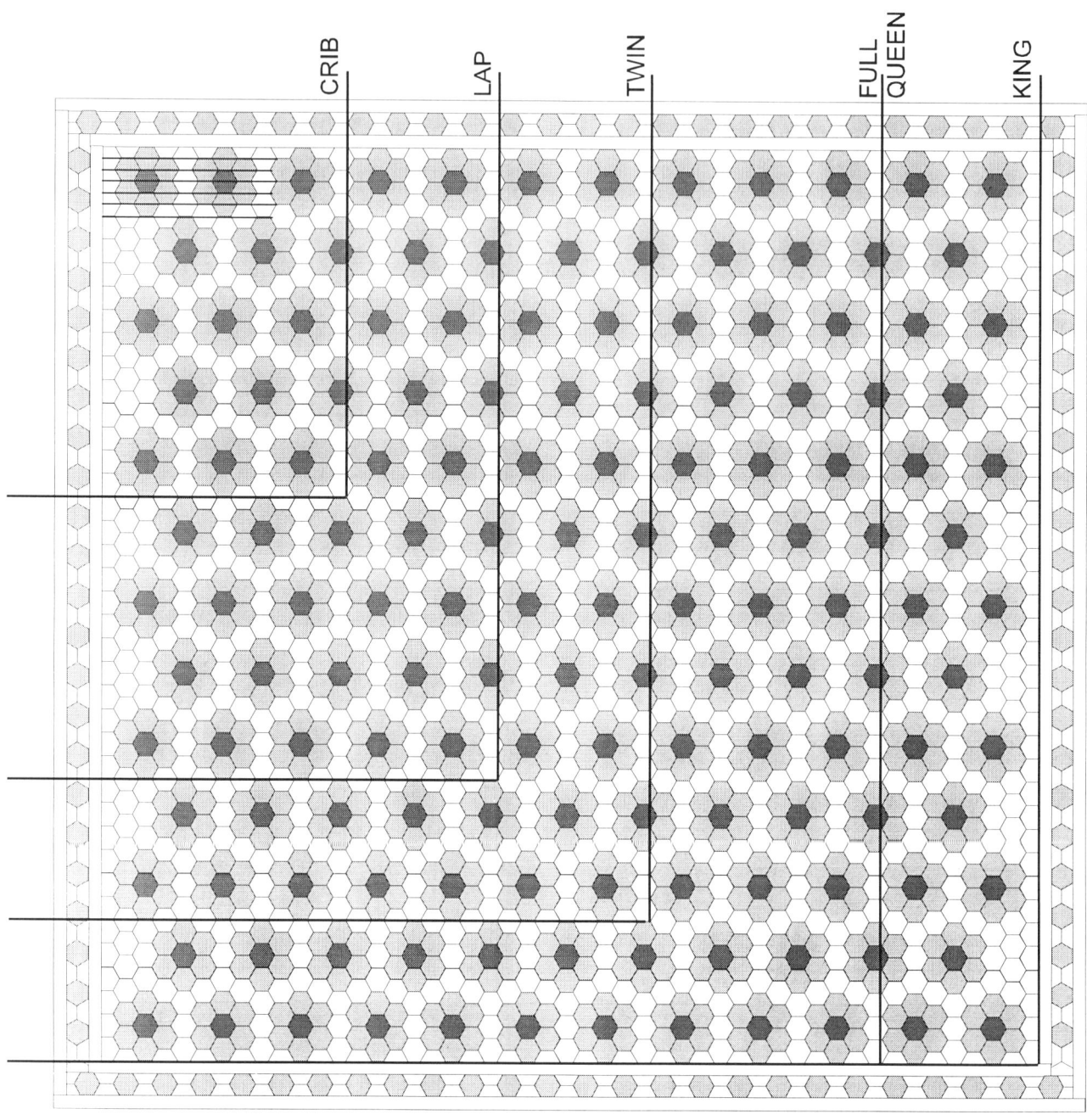

Figure 28 Grandmother's Flower Garden, layout for all sizes

Borders

Stay-stitch the entire quilt slightly outside the line where the binding will be sewn. Use a long acrylic ruler and rotary cutter to trim and straighten the left and right sides.

Measure the length of the quilt in three places. Average the measurements. Sew the border strips together and then cut to this length. Pin in place, ease where necessary, and sew. Measure the width of the quilt in three places, average, and cut the top and bottom borders to this length. Pin, ease, and sew in place.

Using the number of border hexagons listed in Table 2, construct the borders from the remaining half-hexagon pairs. See Figure 29. Apply these borders by measuring, averaging, cutting, pinning, easing and sewing as described for the first border. The sides are sewn on first, then the top and bottom.

The last borders are attached in this same manner using the remainder of border strips. Again, sew on sides then top and bottom.

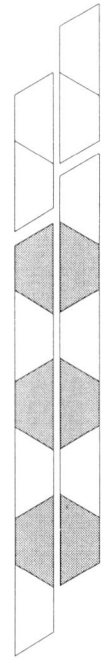

Figure 29

Quilting Designs

Figure 30 shows some ideas for quilting designs. Traditionally the flowers are quilted 1/4" away in each hexagon or as a whole flower. See Figure 23.

Figure 30

75 - Central, Shades Of Construction

Make this scrappy, random quilt using various shades of one color or choose a multiple of colors. Either way, the more variation in value, light to dark, the more dramatic the quilt will be. To make this quilt, read about fabric choices below, then follow the instructions in "The Method" section. Refer to Table 3, the layout diagrams, and the special instructions as needed.

Fabric Choices

The number of fabrics suggested are based on the number and length of strips to be cut from each fabric. To avoid patterns appearing, the number of strips cut is close to the number of fabrics. i.e. 8 strips cut from 10 different fabrics. This way each fabric can be matched up with one of almost every other fabric. With more fabrics and fewer strips cut from each, a pattern can develop as the quilt is laid out.

Table 3 75-Central, Shades of Construction

	CRIB	LAP	TWIN	FULL/QUEEN	KING
Finished Size	27" x 42"	41" x 60"	61" x 86"	88" x 94"	101" x 94"
No. of Hexagons	12 x 21	18 x 30	27 x 43	39 x 47	45 x 47
YARDAGE	Only allows for shrinkage and straightening.				
(No. of fabrics) Yards of Each	(13) 1/4 ea.	(11) 1/2 ea.	(20) 5/8 ea.	(24) 3/4 ea.	(27) 3/4 ea.
Binding	1/3	1/2	5/8	3/4	3/4
Backing	1 1/2	3 1/4	5 1/3	8	9
CUTTING					
Cut this no. of 3"x45" of each fabric	2	5	6	8	8
Cut all strips into: (not an exact measurement)	1/4's (3"x11")	1/2's (3"x22")	1/3's (3"x15")	1/3's (3"x15")	1/3's (3"x15")
Binding 2 1/4"x45"	4	5	8	9	10
BACKING					

The Quilts, 75-Central, Shades of Construction

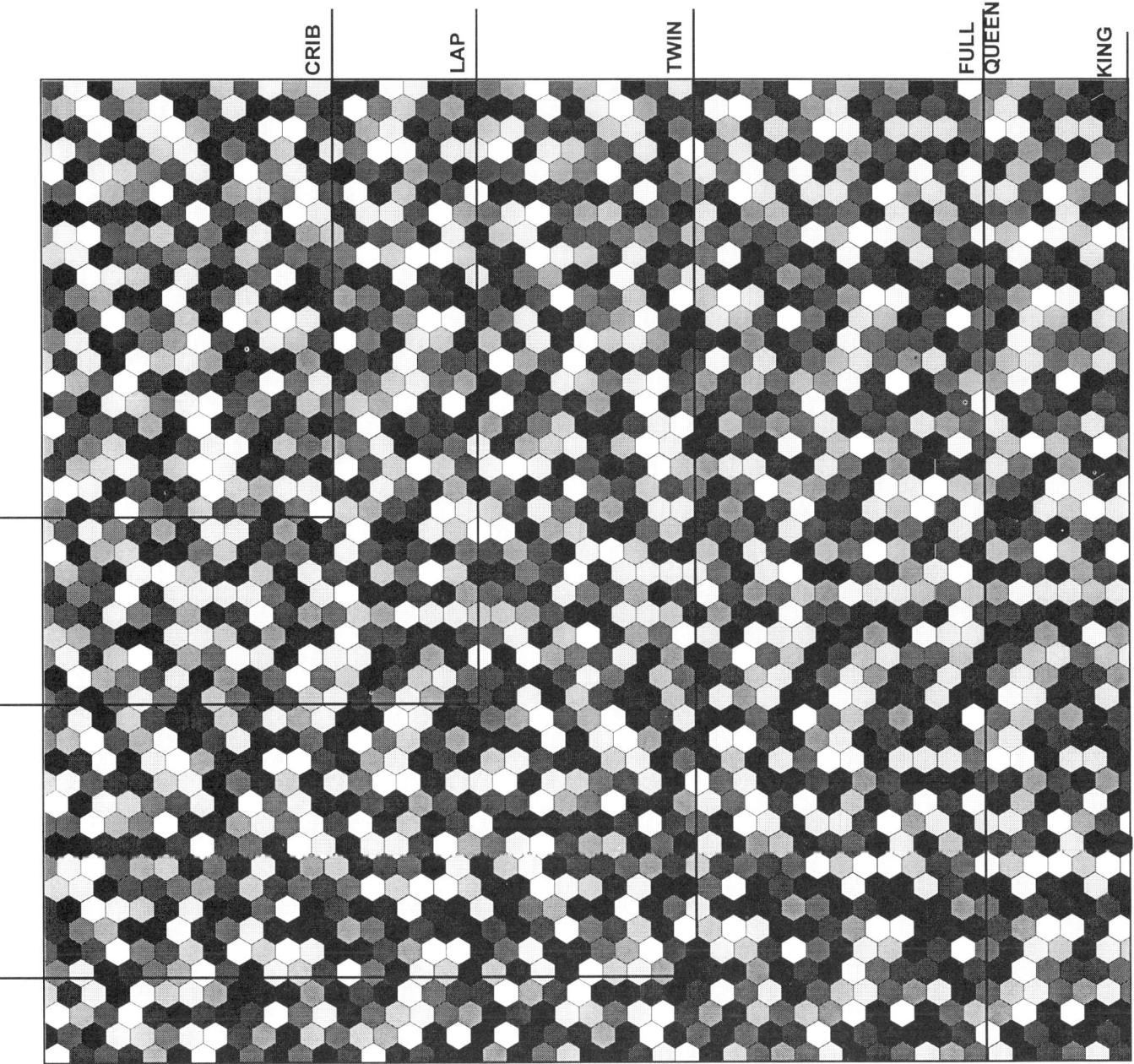

Figure 31

Sewing Strip Pairs

Pair up the fabric strips so that each fabric is matched with each of the others. Do not pair a fabric with itself. For the crib, lap, and king there are not enough strips to make every possible pair, so choose your favorite combinations. For the twin size, the number of strips match exactly to give one of each possible pair. For the full/queen size there is one pair of strips which needs to be repeated, so pair an extra of your choice. Most likely a pattern will not be obvious since the quilt is so large.

The Quilts. 75-Central. Shades of Construction

Layout

This design is worked in diagonal lines even though it is random. Begin at the lower left corner working up and across. See Figure 32. The top and bottom edges are filled in with leftover half-hexagon pairs or with singles, cut from extra fabric.

Quilting Designs

Figure 33 shows the method used for quilting *75-Central*. Using the seams as guides, these lines were quilted without marking. Quilt with the lines running parallel to the seams of the hexagons.

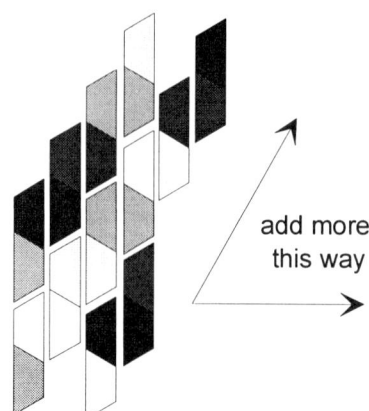

Figure 32

Figure 33

Blue Diamonds

This is a wonderful design that can be simple yet stunning in just three colors. Or make it scrappy for a more homespun feel. Yardages are given for both in Tables 4 and 5. Follow the instructions in "The Method" section, referring back to this table and layout diagram as needed.

Table 4 Blue Diamonds, one diamond fabric

One Diamond Fabric	CRIB	LAP	TWIN	FULL/QUEEN	KING
Finished Size	35" x 54"	55" x 76"	63" x 88"	81" x 95"	100" x 95"
Number of Diamonds	18	44	59	85	105
YARDAGE	Only allows for shrinkage and straightening.				
Center	1/4	1/2	2/3	7/8	1 1/8
Diamonds	1 3/4	4	5 1/4	7	8 3/4
Background	1 3/4	4	5 1/4	7	8 3/4
Binding	3/8	1/2	5/8	2/3	3/4
Backing	1 3/4	3 1/2	5 1/3	7 1/2	8 1/2
CUTTING	Cut number of strips in parentheses.				
Center	(2) 3" x 45"	(5) 3" x 45"	(7) 3" x 45"	(9) 3" x 45"	(12) 3" x 45"
Diamonds Accent border strips	(19) 3"x45" (2) 1 5/8"x45"	(43) 3"x45" (3) 1 5/8"x45"	(56) 3"x45" (4) 1 5/8"x45"	(79) 3"x45" (4) 1 5/8"x45"	(97) 3"x45" (5) 1 5/8"x45"
Background Border strips	(19) 3" x 45" (2) 1 5/8"x45"	(42) 3" x 45" (3) 1 5/8"x45"	(57) 3" x 45" (4) 1 5/8"x45"	(78) 3" x 45" (4) 1 5/8" x 45"	(97) 3" x 45" (5) 1 5/8" x 45"
Binding	(5) 2 1/4"x45"	(7) 2 1/4"x45"	(8) 2 1/4"x45"	(9) 2 1/4"x45"	(10) 2 1/4"x45"
SEWING STRIP PAIRS	Sew number of pairs in parentheses.				
Center to Diamond	(2)	(5)	(7)	(9)	(12)
Diamond to Diamond	(5)	(11)	(14)	(20)	(24)
Diamond to Background	(7)	(16)	(21)	(30)	(37)
Background to Background	(6)	(13)	(18)	(24)	(30)

The Quilts. Blue Diamonds

Table 5 Blue Diamonds, multiple diamond fabrics

Variety of Diamond Fabrics	CRIB	LAP	TWIN	FULL/QUEEN	KING
Finished Size	35" x 54"	55" x 76"	63" x 88"	81" x 95"	100" x 95"
Number of Diamonds	18	44	59	85	105
YARDAGE	Only allows for shrinkage and straightening.				
Center	1/3	1/2	3/4	1	1 1/8
(Number of Diamond Fabrics) Yards of each	(9) 1/3 ea.	(15) 1/3 ea.	(15) 3/8 ea.	(15) 5/8 ea.	(18) 5/8 ea.
Background	2	4 1/4	5	6 3/4	8
Accent Border Strips & Binding	1/2	2/3	3/4	7/8	1
Backing	1 3/4	3 1/2	5 1/3	7 1/2	8 1/2
CUTTING	Cut number of strips in parentheses. 11", 15", and 22" are approximate.				
Center	(9) 3" x 11"	(15) 3" x 15"	(15) 3" x 22"	(30) 3" x 15"	(36) 3" x 15"
Diamonds, each fabric	(1) 3" x 45" (2) 3" x 22" (1) 3" x 11"	(1) 3" x 45" (2) 3" x 30" (2) 3" x 15"	(3) 3" x 45" (2) 3" x 22"	(4) 3" x 45" (4) 3" x 15"	(4) 3" x 45" (4) 3" x 15"
Background	(19) 3" x 45" (2) 3" x 22"	(39) 3" x 45" (15) 3" x 15"	(47) 3" x 45" (17) 3" x 22"	(76) 3" x 45"	(90) 3" x 45" (2) 3" x 22"
Background Border Strips	(2) 1 5/8" x 45"	(3) 1 5/8" x 45"	(4) 1 5/8" x 45"	(4) 1 5/8" x 45"	(5) 1 5/8" x 45"
Accent Border Strips	(2) 1 5/8" x 45"	(3) 1 5/8" x 45"	(4) 1 5/8" x 45"	(4) 1 5/8" x 45"	(5) 1 5/8" x 45"
Binding	(5) 2 1/4" x 45"	(7) 2 1/4" x 45"	(8) 2 1/4" x 45"	(9) 2 1/4" x 45"	(10) 2 1/4" x 45"
SEWING STRIP PAIRS	Sew number of pairs in parentheses at the specified length.				
Center to Each Diamond	(1) 11"	(1) 15"	(1) 22"	(2) 15"	(2) 15"
Each Diamond to itself	(1) 22"	(1) 30"	(1) 45"	(1) 45" (1) 15"	(1) 45" (1) 15"
Each Diamond to Background	(1) 45"	(1) 45"	(1) 45" (1) 22"	(2) 45"	(2) 45"
Background to	(5) 45"	(12) 45" (1) 15"	(16) 45"	(23) 45"	(27) 45"

The Quilts. Blue Diamonds

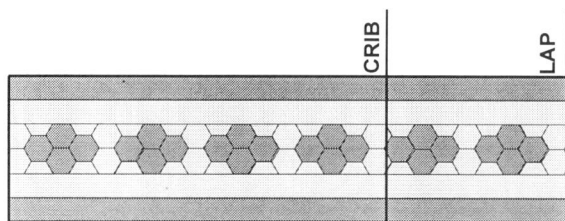

Figure 34

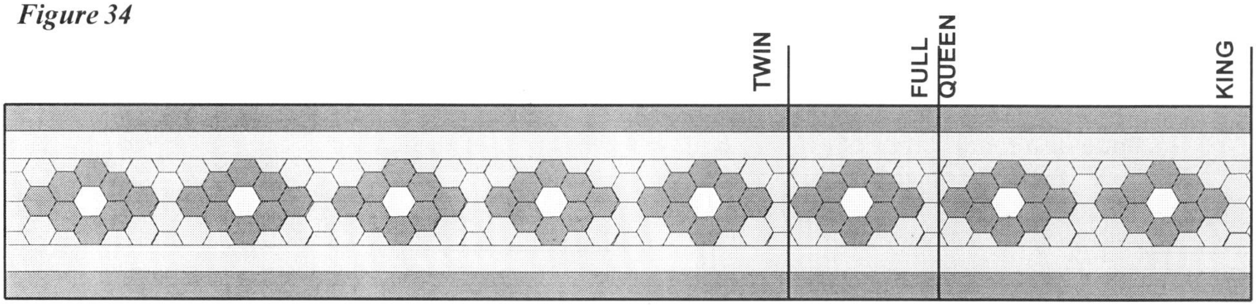

Figure 35

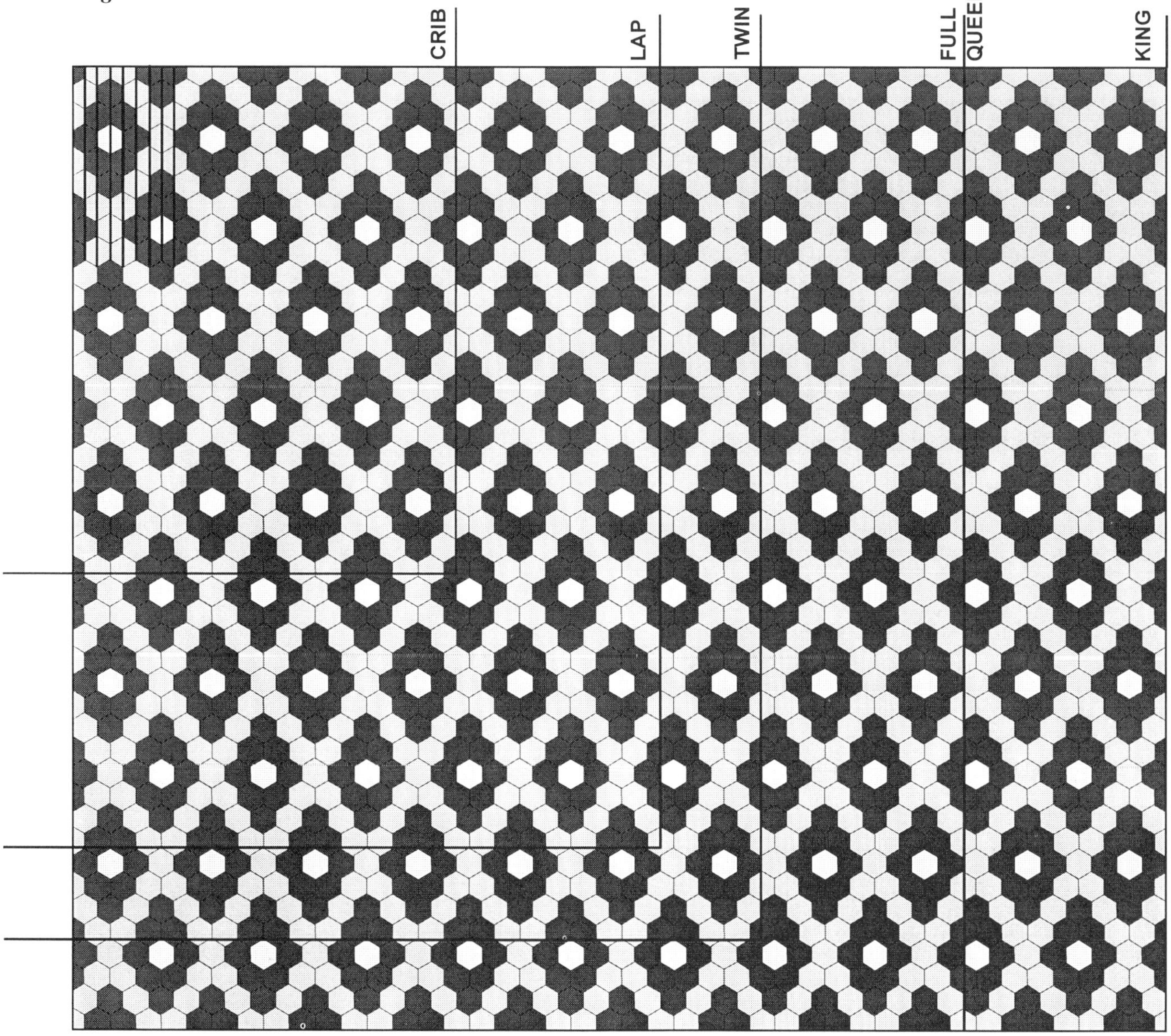

Figure 36

Not Your Grandmother's Flower Garden

The Quilts. Blue Diamonds

Layout

Blue Diamonds has a basic "block" which is repeated. Lay out one diamond following Figure 37. The diamonds fit together like a dovetail joint (as in woodworking) or jigsaw puzzle pieces. Figure 38. This method is different in that the "blocks" are not sewn together but are used only for design. The rows are sewn into strips which lay the length of the quilt, as shown in the upper left hand corner of Figure 36.

Border

Using the number of border diamonds listed in Table 6, construct the top border from the remaining half-hexagon pairs. See Figure 34 for crib and lap sizes. Figure 35 is for twin, full/queen, and king sizes. Add extra background pieces on either end so the border can be trimmed to the proper length.

After stay-stitching the edges, measure the width of the quilt in three places. Average the measurements. Cut the border to this length. Pin in place, ease where necessary, and sew.

Quilting Designs

Figure 39 shows the quilting design used on this quilt.

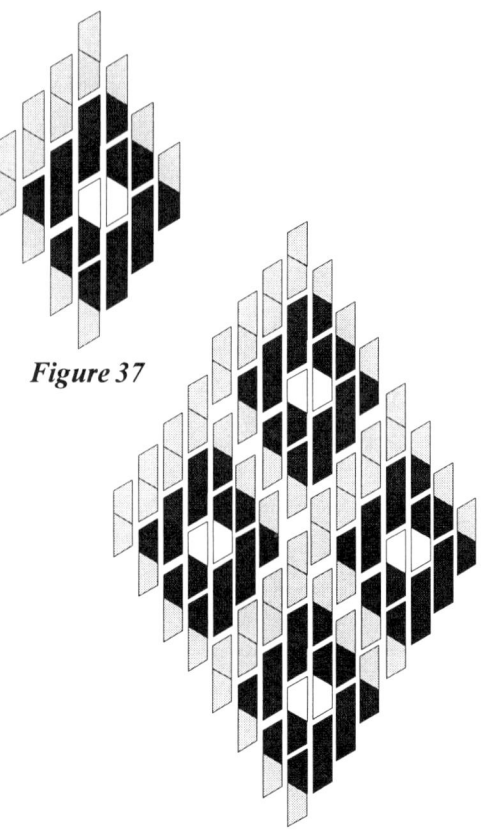

Figure 37

Figure 38

Figure 39

Table 6   Blue Diamonds, single or multiple diamond fabrics

	CRIB	LAP	TWIN	FULL/QUEEN	KING
BORDER					
Number of Diamonds	4	6	5	6	8
Size of Diamonds	Small	Small	Large	Large	Large
BACKING					

Mosaic Trip Around the World

Make the traditional Trip-Around-the-World but with a new angle. Use a wide selection of light, medium and dark fabrics to give movement and depth to the quilt. For this project, use Table 7, the layout diagram, and quilting designs as referred to from "The Method" section.

Layout

For this design, begin in the middle, work from the center out, one fourth of the quilt at a time. Figure 40. The rows are sewn into strips which lay the length of the quilt. Figure 41 shows the crib size layout. Figure 42 shows lap size. Figure 43 is for twin, full/queen, and king.

Quilting Designs

The center portion of Figure 41 shows the quilting design used. No marking is required and the diamond shape is reinforced.

Figure 40

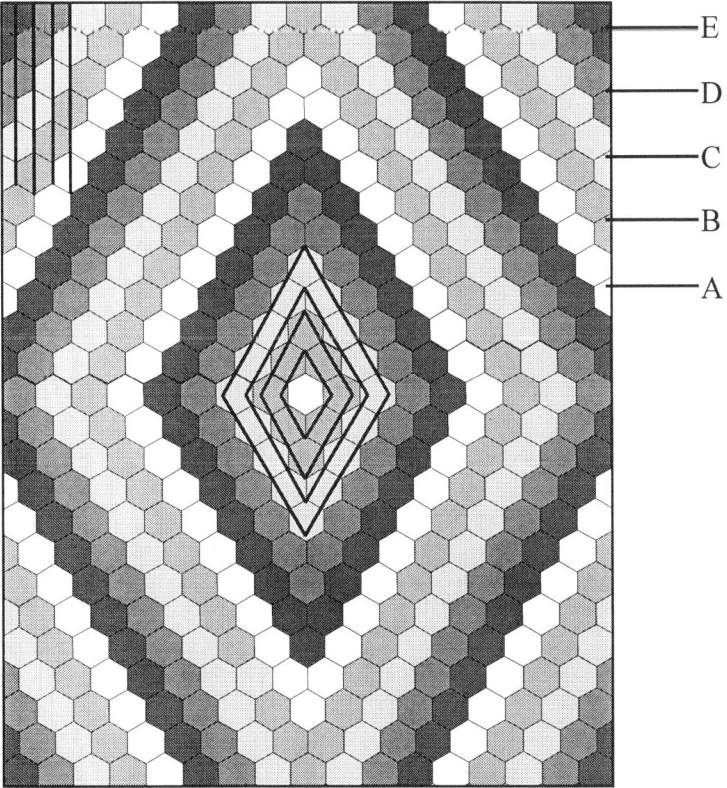

Figure 41 Mosaic Trip Around the World, crib size

The Quilts. Mosaic Trip Around the World

Table 7 Mosaic Trip Around the World

	CRIB	LAP	TWIN	FULL/QUEEN	KING
Finished Size	40" x 50"	52" x 74"	56" x 89"	88" x 97"	97" x 97"
YARDAGE	Only allows for shrinkage and straightening.				
Number of Fabrics	5 (A-E)	7 (A-G)	9 (A-I)	9 (A-I)	9 (A-I)
Yards of each	1 ea.	1 1/4 ea.	1 5/8 ea.	2 ea.	2 1/4 ea.
Binding	3/8	1/2	5/8	3/4	3/4
CUTTING	Cut number of strips in parentheses. 11", 15", and 22" are approximate.				
A	(8) 3" x 45" (2) 3" x 15"	(12) 3" x 45"	(16) 3" x 45" (1) 3" x 11"	(20) 3" x 45" (4) 3" x 11"	(21) 3" x 45" (3) 3" x 22"
B	(8) 3" x 45" (4) 3" x 15"	(12) 3" x 45" (1) 3" x 15"	(16) 3" x 45" (1) 3" x 22" (3) 3" x 11"	(20) 3" x 45" (4) 3" x 11"	(24) 3" x 45"
C	(8) 3" x 45" (4) 3" x 15"	(12) 3" x 45" (4) 3" x 15"	(16) 3" x 45" (4) 3" x 22"	(20) 3" x 45" (4) 3" x 11"	(24) 3" x 45"
D	(8) 3" x 45" (4) 3" x 15"	(12) 3" x 45" (4) 3" x 15"	(16) 3" x 45" (4) 3" x 22"	(20) 3" x 45" (4) 3" x 11"	(24) 3" x 45"
E	(8) 3" x 45" (4) 3" x 15"	(12) 3" x 45" (4) 3" x 15"	(16) 3" x 45" (4) 3" x 22"	(20) 3" x 45" (4) 3" x 11"	(24) 3" x 45"
F	-	(12) 3" x 45" (1) 3" x 15"	(16) 3" x 45" (1) 3" x 22" (3) 3" x 11"	(20) 3" x 45" (4) 3" x 11"	(24) 3" x 45"
G	-	(12) 3" x 45" (1) 3" x 15"	(16) 3" x 45" (1) 3" x 11"	(20) 3" x 45" (4) 3" x 11"	(21) 3" x 45" (3) 3" x 22"
H	-	-	(16) 3" x 45"	(20) 3" x 45" (4) 3" x 11"	(20) 3" x 45" (4) 3" x 22"
I	-	-	(16) 3" x 45"	(20) 3" x 45" (4) 3" x 11"	(20) 3" x 45" (4) 3" x 22"

Cut and paste scraps of each fabric for reference while cutting and sewing.

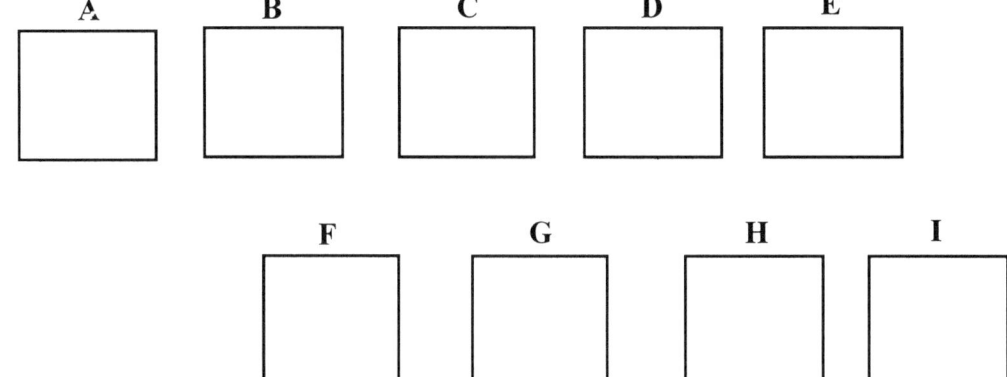

Not Your Grandmother's Flower Garden

Table 7 Mosaic Trip Around the World, continued

	CRIB	LAP	TWIN	FULL/QUEEN	KING
SEWING STRIP PAIRS					
A - A	(2) 45"	(3) 45"	(4) 45"	(5) 45", (1) 11"	(5) 45", (1) 22"
A - B	(2) 45", (1) 15"	(3) 45"	(4) 45", (1) 11"	(5) 45", (1) 11"	(6) 45"
B - B	(2) 45", (1) 15"	(3) 45"	(4) 45", (1) 11"	(5) 45", (1) 11"	(6) 45"
B - C	(2) 45", (1) 15"	(3) 45", (1) 15"	(4) 45", (1) 22"	(5) 45", (1) 11"	(6) 45"
C - C	(2) 45", (1) 15"	(3) 45", (1) 15"	(4) 45", (1) 22"	(5) 45", (1) 11"	(6) 45"
C - D	(2) 45", (1) 15"	(3) 45", (1) 15"	(4) 45", (1) 22"	(5) 45", (1) 11"	(6) 45"
D - D	(2) 45", (1) 15"	(3) 45", (1) 15"	(4) 45", (1) 22"	(5) 45", (1) 11"	(6) 45"
D - E	(2) 45", (1) 15"	(3) 45", (1) 15"	(4) 45", (1) 22"	(5) 45", (1) 11"	(6) 45"
E - E	(2) 45", (1) 15"	(3) 45", (1) 15"	(4) 45", (1) 22"	(5) 45", (1) 11"	(6) 45"
E - F, E-A for crib	(2) 45", (1) 15"	(3) 45", (1) 15"	(4) 45", (1) 22"	(5) 45", (1) 11"	(6) 45"
F - F	-	(3) 45", (1) 15"	(4) 45", (1) 11"	(5) 45", (1) 11"	(6) 45"
F - G	-	(3) 45", (1) 15"	(4) 45", (1) 11"	(5) 45", (1) 11"	(6) 45"
G - G	-	(3) 45"	(4) 45"	(5) 45", (1) 11"	(5) 45", (1) 22"
G - H, G-A for lap	-	(3) 45"	(4) 45"	(5) 45", (1) 11"	(5) 45", (1) 22"
H - H	-	-	(4) 45"	(5) 45", (1) 11"	(5) 45", (1) 22"
H - I	-	-	(4) 45"	(5) 45", (1) 11"	(5) 45", (1) 22"
I - I	-	-	(4) 45"	(5) 45", (1) 11"	(5) 45", (1) 22"
I - A	-	-	(4) 45"	(5) 45", (1) 11"	(5) 45", (1) 22"

The Quilts, Mosaic Trip Around the World

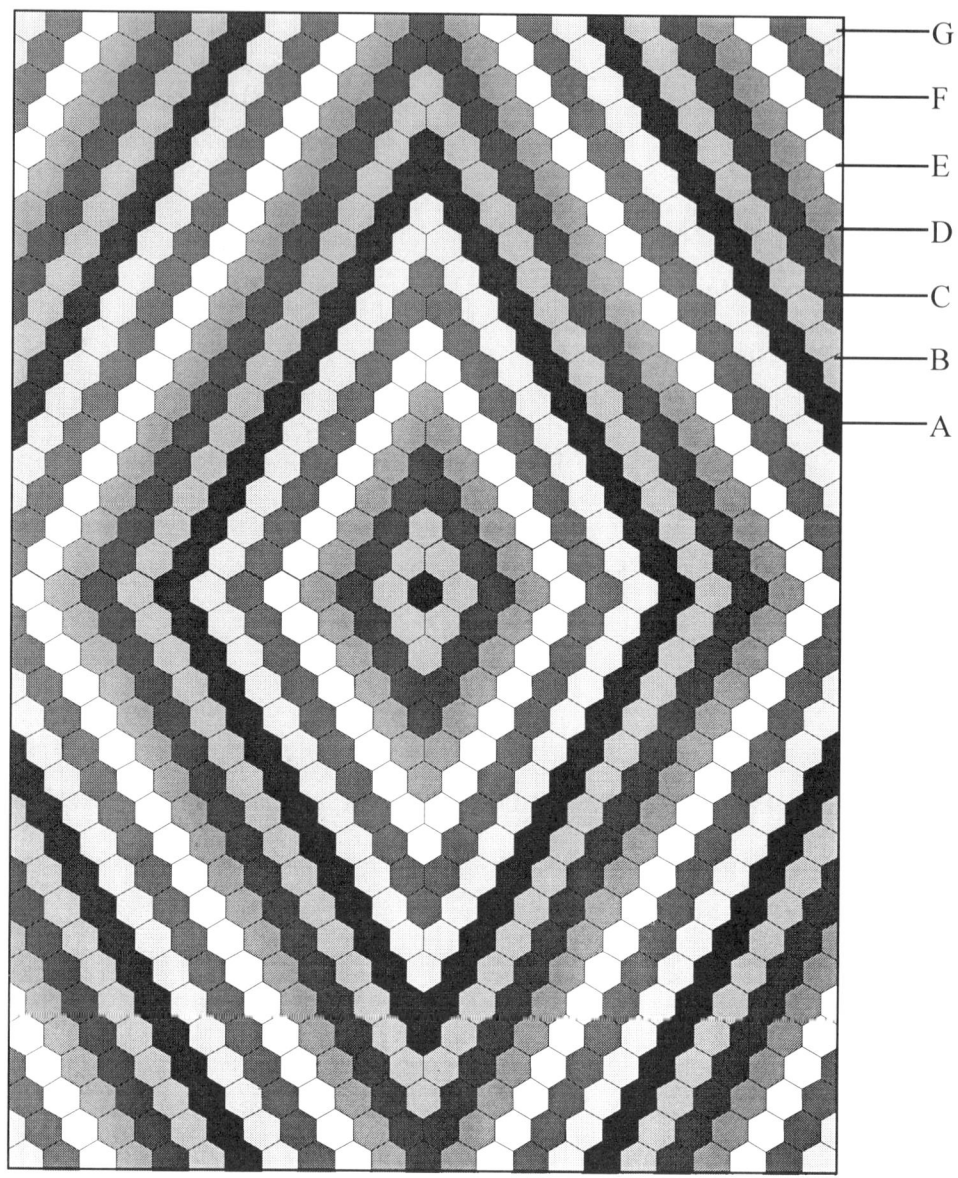

Figure 42 Mosaic Trip Around the World, lap size

Table 7 Mosaic Trip Around the World, continued

	CRIB	LAP	TWIN	FULL/QUEEN	KING
Binding, cut strips	(5) 2 1/4"x45"	(7) 2 1/4"x45"	(8) 2 1/4"x45"	(10) 2 1/4"x45"	(10) 2 1/4"x45"
BACKING					

Not Your Grandmother's Flower Garden

The Quilts. Mosaic Trip Around the World

Figure 43 Mosaic Trip Around the World, twin, full/queen, king size

Not Your Grandmother's Flower Garden

Some Basics

Warning! The rotary cutter is very sharp and should be handled with care. Always close the blade cover after each cut!

How to use a Rotary Cutter, Ruler, and Mat

When using a rotary cutter and mat, fold the fabric with wrong sides together, selvage to selvage, so the fabric lays flat from the fold to the selvages. Always cut one direction with the rotary cutter, not back and forth. (I prefer away from myself.) Lay the ruler on the fabric, aligning the fold with a rule line. Figure 44. Hold the ruler firm using your fingertips and cut the fabric under the portion of the ruler held by your hand. Leaving the cutter in place, walk your hand up the ruler and keep the ruler still. Continue the cut. By making the cut in several smaller motions, you are less likely to have the ruler slip.

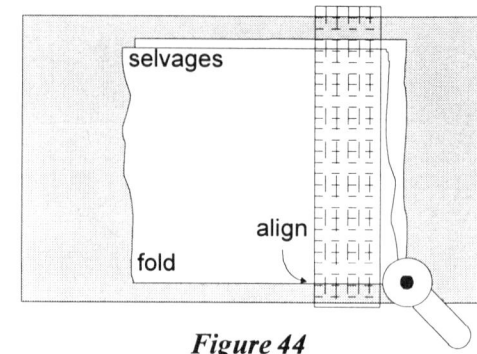

Figure 44

If the cutting mat or ruler is not long enough, fold the fabric again with the single fold covering the selvages. It is most important that the folds are parallel to each other and the ruler lines. Figure 45. The selvages and end will probably be a little crooked and that's okay. Line up the double fold with an inch mark on the mat or ruler. Now check that the single fold is an equal amount away from the nearest inch line. If it is not even, you need to adjust by moving the corner which is higher down, and the lower corner up.

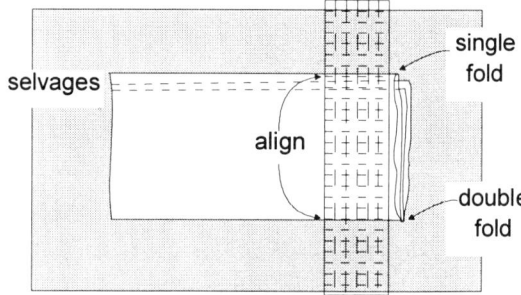

Figure 45

Trim the ragged edge. Move the ruler and cut the desired width of strip. With each cut, make sure the fabric is flat and the folds are parallel to the ruler lines.

Basting

Cut the backing about 3" larger than the quilt top, on each side. Using masking tape, attach the backing fabric to the floor or table with right side down. Figure 46.

Figure 46

Cut the batting about 2" larger than the quilt top on each side. Lay batting on top of backing, smoothing out any wrinkles. Lay out the quilt top, right side up, centering it on the backing.

To begin a basting stitch, take several overlapping stitches in different directions. Figure 47. This will hold it tight enough so knots are not necessary. Hand baste with a large running stitch through all three layers about every 3 - 4", following

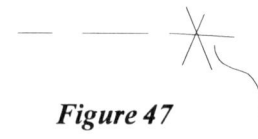

Figure 47

Some Basics

the grid pattern in Figure 48. Remove the tape. Fold backing around to front, covering batting, hand baste in place. This will keep the batting from catching on everything while quilting.

Quilting

Place the section to be quilted in a quilting hoop. The quilt should be loose enough to rock the needle up and down. Thread a between needle (size 9, 10, 11 or 12) with 18"-24" of quilting thread. Knot one end. Put the needle in about $1/2$" away from the beginning of the quilting line. Going through only the top layer and batting, bring the needle up at the starting point. Pull gently until the knot pops through the top layer and is hidden in the batting. Figure 49. Now make a running stitch through all three layers following the quilting design. Figure 50. Keep the stitches straight and even before attempting small ones. Smaller stitches come with practice. To end the thread, make a knot just above the surface of the quilt. Take one more stitch through the top and batting only. Pull gently until the knot is in the batting.

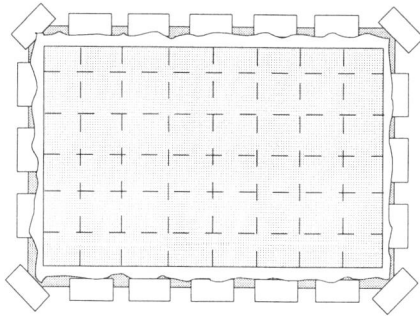

Figure 48

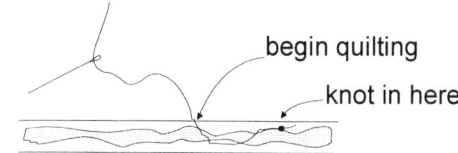

Figure 49

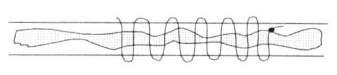

Figure 50

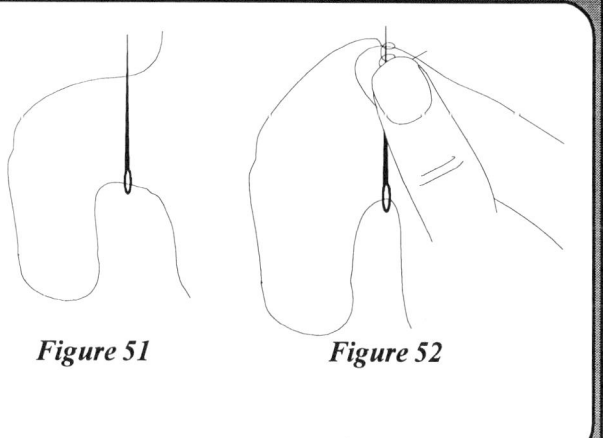

HINT: Quilter's Knot

Make a quilter's knot by placing the end of the thread across the needle. While holding it down between your thumb and forefinger, Figure 51, wrap the thread closest to the tip of the needle around the needle 2 or 3 times. Holding the wrapped thread securely between your thumb and forefinger, pull the needle up until the length of thread has slipped through your fingers, leaving a consistently-sized knot at the end Figure 52.

Figure 51 *Figure 52*

Binding

Sew binding strips together, end to end. Fold the binding in half lengthwise with wrong sides together and pin it to the top of the quilt with the raw edges of the binding $1/4$" outside the sewing line. (This is usually the edge of the quilt top.) Figure 53. Leave 6"-8" loose at this end for finishing. Sew with $1/4$" seam through all layers, back stitching at the beginning.

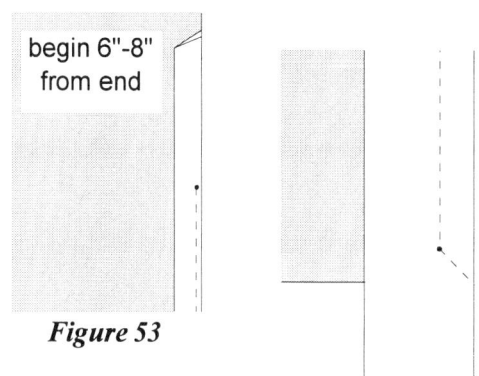

Figure 53

Figure 54

Some Basics

To miter the corner, stop with the needle down 1/4" away from the end and pivot on the diagonal. Sew to the corner. Figure 54. Fold the binding back along the sewn diagonal line. Figure 55. Now fold the binding down having the fold 1/4" into the seam allowance. The loose binding now lines up with the next edge to be sewn. Figure 56.

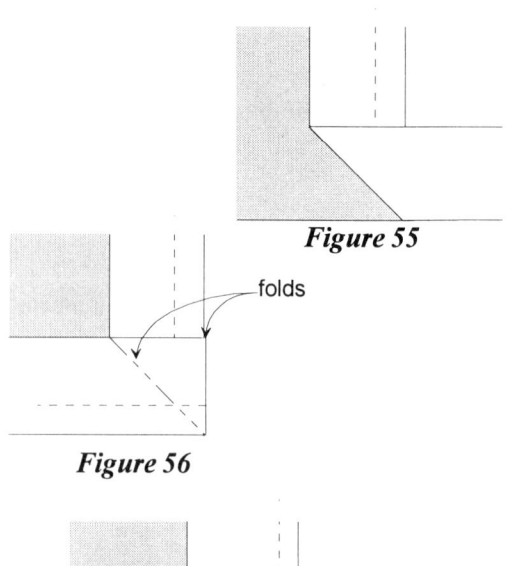

Figure 55

Figure 56

> **HINT: Wider Bindings**
>
> *If you are making 1/4" finished binding, the fold should match up with the raw edge of the binding. For larger bindings, the fold should be the finished width of the binding into the seam allowance. Figure 57.*

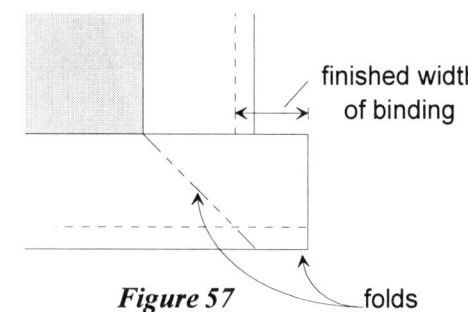

Figure 57

Sew from the fold down to the next corner with 1/4" seam. Continue binding and mitering each corner, stopping about 8" from the starting point. Backstitch and remove the quilt from the sewing machine.

The binding is finished by sewing the two ends together so the binding will lay flat. Unfold the binding. Lay each binding end flat along the quilt until they meet halfway. With the binding ends right sides together, insert a pin 1/4" in from the edge of the binding through both ends of the binding. Figure 58. Keeping only this point constant, rotate the binding ends so they lay across each other at an angle (any angle). Figure 59. Pin in place making sure the original point is still matched. Sew in a straight line from one edge where the binding ends meet to the other edge where they meet. Make sure the quilt is on one side of this line and the loose ends are on the other. Check that the binding lays flat along the quilt, then trim ends to 1/4" seam allowance. Now fold binding in half and finish sewing it to the quilt with 1/4" seam.

Trim the excess batting and backing to 1/4". Fold the binding around to the back and hand stitch using a blind, ladder or applique stitch. At the corners, fold down the right side, then the left side to evenly distribute the bulk. Figure 60.

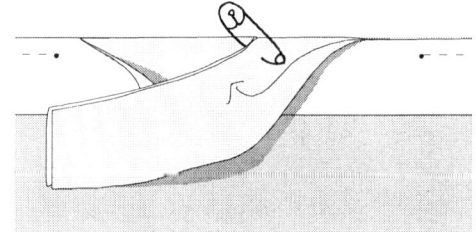

Figure 58

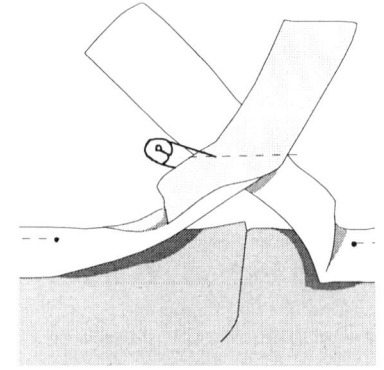

Figure 59

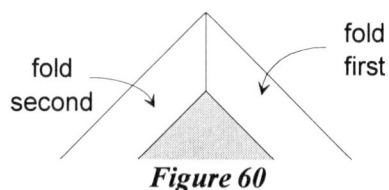

Figure 60